Will There Be Knights and Dragons?

A Children's Book about Windsor Castle

Written by Marion McAuley and Leah Kharibian

Illustrated by Katy Sleight

ROYAL COLLECTION PUBLICATIONS

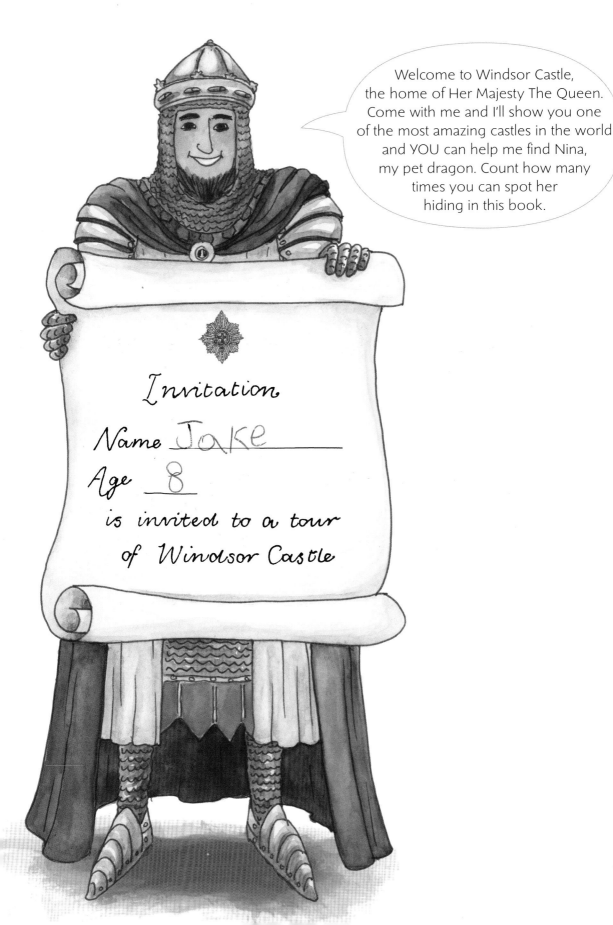

CONTENTS

WHERE IS WINDSOR CASTLE?

Windsor Castle is the oldest, largest and most famous royal castle in the world. It is one of The Queen's favourite homes. The Castle is 23 miles from London and is built on a high hill near the River Thames. The Queen spends the month around Easter, a week in June and many of her weekends at the Castle. If she is at home, you will see a flag called the Royal Standard flying above the Round Tower.

The Union flag, often known as the Union Jack, is flown when The Queen is away.

River Thames

St George's Chap

Look! The Royal Standard is flying above the Round Tower. It shows that The Queen is home.

But where's the dragon?

Round Tower

Upper Ward

Home Park

To London

THE STRONGEST CASTLE

Windsor Castle was built nearly 1,000 years ago by a king called William the Conqueror. The Castle was built to protect the king from his enemies. William chose the big hill at Windsor because fortresses that are built on hills are hard to attack. To make his castle even more difficult to attack, William had a huge mound of earth put on top of the hill. Then on top of that, he built the strongest part of the Castle. It's called a 'keep'.

Windsor Castle was first built of wood, but over time the wood was replaced by strong stone. Some walls are 4 metres thick!

ATTACK! ATTACK!

Windsor Castle has only been attacked three times. Eight hundred years ago, the armies of important men tried to break into the Castle because they were not happy with the king, who was called John. But King John's soldiers had many ways to keep them away. Archers inside the Castle could fire arrows through narrow openings in the walls, called arrow loops, and soldiers could drop boiling water, hot oil and rocks through 'murder holes.' These were built above the strong stone gateways.

This secret passage runs under the Castle. It was built so people could come and go without being seen by enemies.

9

Those hats with feathers are great!

KNIGHTS AND DRAGONS

Yes, there are knights and dragons at Windsor Castle! For over 650 years the Castle has been the meeting place for special knights belonging to a group called the Order of the Garter. The Order was started by a king called Edward III. At this time, when people began something new, they often chose a saint to guard over their plans from heaven. Edward chose a brave knight, St George, and the beautiful chapel inside the Castle became known as St George's Chapel.

One story about St George tells how he rescued a princess from being eaten by a fierce dragon! Sculptures of George and the dragon are all over the Castle.

11

SHINING ARMOUR

Hundreds of years ago, knights came from far and wide to Windsor Castle to take part in fighting competitions known as jousts. Although the knights used blunt weapons and wore armour and held shields to protect themselves, many were hurt and some were killed. It was a very dangerous sport! Inside Windsor Castle there are many suits of armour that were especially made for jousting.

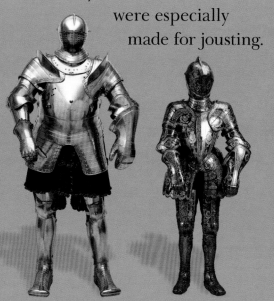

The suit of armour on the left was made for King Henry VIII. It shows he was very tall as well as big around the tummy. The suit on the right was made for a 14-year-old prince.

Suits of armour were carefully made to fit like the very best clothes.

Although The Queen doesn't sleep in this bed, important guests have slept here in the past.

Windsor Castle is divided into several parts called wards. There are 951 rooms in the Upper Ward and 225 of those are bedrooms. The best rooms are called the State Apartments. In the past, kings and queens met visitors, ate, danced and slept in these rooms. The State Apartments are still used to entertain important guests, but today The Queen lives in private rooms in another part of the Castle. She holds special sleepovers at the Castle, which are called 'dine and sleep'.

Each room in the Castle is beautifully decorated. These winged children with loaves of bread are painted onto the ceiling of the King's Dining Room.

WITH WONDERFUL TREASURES!

The State Apartments are full of amazing paintings, sculptures, clocks and glittering chandeliers. This is because every king and queen for the last 500 years has added to the collection! Today the Castle is like the very best museum and art gallery rolled into one. The Queen makes sure all these treasures are carefully looked after so that everybody can enjoy them, now and in the future.

This table is made from silver and is over 300 years old! When it was made people were very excited about a new type of fruit that had arrived from abroad. Can you guess what it was?

The boy in the centre of this painting grew up to be a king. As Charles II, he was one of the kings who did most to make Windsor Castle a splendid palace.

The Queen's favourite dogs are corgis and dorgis. She travels everywhere with them, unless she is abroad. The dogs often get walked in these gardens.

Windsor is a great place to have fun. In the past, the royal forests and parks around the Castle were used for hunting, riding and archery. Over time, the land was also used to create gardens, farms and even a zoo! Today, outdoor life is still important. The Queen and members of the Royal Family all enjoy riding their horses and spending time with their pets.

The Queen learnt to ride as a child. Here she is with her pony Hans after they won a cup at the first Royal Windsor Horse Show in 1944.

THE BEST DOLLS' HOUSE

Almost 100 years ago, a wonderful dolls' house was made for The Queen's grandmother, Queen Mary. This queen loved collecting beautiful things and so more than 1,000 British craftsmen came together to make her a very special present. However, the dolls' house they built was not made as a toy, it was made for people to admire. It has electric lighting, two working lifts, hot and cold running water, flushing lavatories and a garage full of smart cars!

Everything inside the dolls' house is twelve times smaller than the real thing. This crown is not much bigger than a 50p piece but it is made using real diamonds and rubies.

I wish I was small enough to live here!

The Dolls' House is like a mini palace. This is the Queen's Bedroom.

21

LIFE AT THE CASTLE

Over 160 people live at the Castle, including children! Their homes are built into the Castle's walls, towers and gateways. Lots of people take part in Castle life, too. In St George's Chapel, boys aged between seven and thirteen sing at religious services five days a week. There are also housekeepers, florists, gardeners, postmen, chefs, policemen, librarians, priests, musicians and retired soldiers known as Military Knights. There is also a

special person called the flagman. His job is to raise the flag on the Round Tower.

One of the Royal Clockmakers looks after the Castle's 455 clocks. Some of them are very difficult to reach!

GUARDING THE CASTLE

Windsor Castle is protected day and night by soldiers called Guardsmen. These Guardsmen have their base at the barracks in Windsor town. When new Guardsmen arrive to take over from the Old Guard at the Castle, there's a ceremony called 'Changing of the Guard'. The new Guardsmen march through Windsor town and then into the Castle, where their Captain is given the keys to the Castle.

At Changing of the Guard, a band leads the way. Sometimes the band plays pop songs or themes from TV!

In my day, a favourite dish made here was stuffed peacock.

A GREAT KITCHEN

The royal kitchen at Windsor Castle is called the Great Kitchen. It is not only very big, it is very old, too. For over 600 years, delicious food has been cooked here for kings, queens, important guests and royal staff. Today the kitchen is full of the latest equipment, although some of the copper pots and pans in use are over 200 years old. Sometimes, when there is an important dinner, the royal chefs have to cook for over 200 guests.

Compared to a normal-size mixer, the Great Kitchen's mixer is enormous! It can whisk 500 eggs at once.

A MAGNIFICENT FEAST

A visit from the leader of another country is celebrated with a magnificent feast called a State Banquet. Before the guests arrive the Castle is very busy. It takes two whole days to lay the enormous table for up to 160 guests. Each place-setting is laid out with all the knives, forks and spoons needed for four separate courses (including pudding AND dessert) as well as six glasses for drinks. That's 1,280 pieces of cutlery and 960 glasses to put out!

Everything is carefully laid out using rulers. The table is 53 metres long – the same as six buses parked end to end.

Mr Knight, I think I've found your dragon!

THE BIGGEST CELEBRATION

When a king or queen reigns for a very long time the whole country has a celebration called a Royal Jubilee. The Diamond Jubilee in 2012 celebrates 60 years of The Queen's reign. Everyone is given a special holiday and people across the United Kingdom and abroad join in the celebrations by holding street parties and lighting a type of fire called a beacon.

Princess Elizabeth became Queen in 1952 when her father died. On 2 June 1953 she was crowned in a special ceremony called a Coronation. This took place at Westminster Abbey.

Look at **www.royalcollection.org.uk**
for information about visiting Windsor Castle,
Buckingham Palace and the Palace of Holyroodhouse.

If you like singing and want to know more about
joining the choir at St George's Chapel visit
www.stgeorges-windsor.org

Look at **www.royal.gov.uk** for information about
The Queen and the British Monarchy.

Written by Marion McAuley and Leah Kharibian
Published by Royal Collection Trust/
© HM Queen Elizabeth II 2012

014098

ISBN 978 1 905686 72 8

British Library Cataloguing in Publication Data: A catalogue
record for this book is available from the British Library.

Designer: Daniel Devlin
Editorial Consultant: Susie Behar
Project Manager: Leah Kharibian
Project Assistant: Nina Chang
Production Manager: Debbie Wayment
Printed on 170gsm Greencoat Silk
Printed and bound by Swallowtail Press Ltd

PICTURE CREDITS

All works reproduced are in the Royal Collection unless
indicated below. The Royal Collection is grateful for
permission to reproduce the following:

pp. 6, 9 photographer: Daniel Devlin
pp. 8, 11, 22 © The Dean & Canons of Windsor
pp. 10, 25, 28, 29 photographer: Ian Jones
p. 13 photographer: Mark Fiennes
pp. 15, 21 photographer: G Newbury
p. 18 photographer: Philip Craven
p. 19 Studio Lisa/© Getty Images
p. 20 photographer: David Cripps
p. 24 photographer: Eva Zielinska-Millar
p. 30 PA Photos/photographer Steve Parsons

Every effort has been made to contact copyright holders;
any omissions are inadvertent and will be corrected in future
editions if notification of the amended credit is sent to the
publisher in writing.

ACKNOWLEDGEMENTS

The permission of Her Majesty The Queen to reproduce items
from the Royal Collection is gratefully acknowledged.

In preparation of this book the authors are indebted to many
colleagues for their assistance including Alison Campbell, Zaki
Cooper, Mark Flanagan, Will Graham, Edward Griffiths, Jacky
Colliss Harvey, Katie Holyoak, Karen Lawson, Charlotte Manley,
Catherine Martin, Simon Metcalf, Daniel Partridge, Stephen
Patterson, Jane Roberts, Penny Russell and Elizabeth Simpson.

We would also like to thank the teachers and pupils of Abbeyhill
Primary School, Barrow Hill Junior School and Montem Primary
School, as well as Albert Cameron and Zara Zafar, for their valuable
comments during the development of this book.

I hope you've had a wonderful time visiting Windsor Castle. Thank you so much for finding Nina. How many times did you spot her?

WORLD
LAND
TRUST™

www.carbonbalancedpaper.com
CBP00013552902124339

She can be seen 19 times.